History's GREATEST RIVALS

SITTING BULL Vs. GEORGE ARMSTRONG CUSTER

THE BATTLE OF THE LITTLE BIGHORN

Ellis Roxburgh

Gareth Stevens PUBLISHING

Please visit our website, **www.garethstevens.com**.
For a free color catalog of all our high-quality books,
call toll-free 1-800-542-2595 or fax 1-877-542-2596.

Library of Congress Cataloging-in-Publication Data

Roxburgh, Ellis.
 Sitting Bull vs. George Armstrong Custer : the Battle of the Little Bighorn / Ellis
Roxburgh.
     pages cm. — (History's greatest rivals)
 Includes index.
 ISBN 978-1-4824-4235-9 (pbk.)
 ISBN 978-1-4824-4236-6 (6 pack)
 ISBN 978-1-4824-4237-3 (library binding)
 1. Little Bighorn, Battle of the, Mont., 1876—Juvenile literature. 2. Custer, George A.
(George Armstrong), 1839-1876—Juvenile literature. 3. Sitting Bull, 1831-1890—Juvenile
literature. I. Title.
 E83.876.R69 2016
 973.8'2—dc23

                        2015024358

Published in 2016 by
Gareth Stevens Publishing
111 East 14th Street, Suite 349
New York, NY 10003

Copyright © 2016 Brown Bear Books Ltd
For Brown Bear Books Ltd:
Editorial Director: Lindsey Lowe
Managing Editor: Tim Cooke
Children's Publisher: Anne O'Daly
Design Manager: Keith Davis
Designer: Lynne Lennon
Picture Manager: Sophie Mortimer

Picture Credits: T=Top, C=Center, B=Bottom, L=Left, R=Right. Front Cover: Library of
Congress: r, background; NARA: l. Art Archive: DEA Picture Library 18; Library of Congress:
1l, 4-5, 7, 10, 11, 13, 16, 20, 27, 28, 31, 32, 34, 37, 38, 41; Museum Syndicate: David Frances Barry
14; NARA: 15, 19, 23, 24, 25, 40; Nordamerika Native Museum: 26; Robert Hunt Library: 12,
39; Shutterstock: Everett Historical 17, 35, Jim Parkin 21; Thinkstock: Photos.com 6, 9, 29, 33;
Topfoto: The Granger Collection 22; Trout Gallery: 34; United States Federal Government:
30; US National Archives: 30 17: Walters Art Museum: 8.

Brown Bear Books has made every attempt to contact the copyright holder. If anyone
has any information please contact licensing@brownbearbooks.co.uk

Manufactured in the United States of America

CPSIA compliance information: Batch #CW16GS. For further information contact
Gareth Stevens, New York, New York at 1-800-542-2595.

CONTENTS

AT ODDS

In the 1860s, Sitting Bull (c. 1831–1890) became the supreme chief of the entire Sioux nation. The title was created especially for him.

* Sitting Bull was 10 years old when he killed his first buffalo.

* He gained his first victory by touching an enemy warrior in battle at age 14.

* Sitting Bull became a spiritual and military leader for the Sioux.

* He brought together the Sioux, North Cheyenne, and Arapaho to resist government pressure to give up land.

4

General George Armstrong Custer (1839–1876) served in the US Army in the Civil War (1861–1865). After the war, he remained in the army. He wanted to become America's leading "Indian fighter."

* Custer graduated at the bottom of his 1861 class at the US Military Academy at West Point.

* In 1863, Custer became the US Army's youngest brigadier general, at just 23 years old.

* In April 1865, Custer, as a Union cavalry commander, accepted the first flag of surrender from Confederate forces.

* On the eve of the Battle of the Little Bighorn, Custer was the most famous and popular soldier in the United States.

CONTEXT

In the early 19th century, groups of Native Americans roamed freely across the Great Plains. Their existence depended on hunting buffalo for food and clothing.

The Sioux Nation lived around the lakes near the source of the Mississippi River in Minnesota. There were three main groups of Sioux: the Santee, or Eastern Dakota; the Yankton-Yanktonai, or Western Dakota; and the Lakota, or Teton, Sioux.

The Sioux were nomadic. They were outstanding hunters, who followed herds of buffalo across the plains. The buffalo provided a ready supply of meat and skins, or hides, to make clothing and tents

HUNT: The Sioux hunted buffalo on horseback. They shot them using bows and arrows or drove them over cliffs to their deaths.

DEATH: A group of Sioux gather for the funeral of a dead warrior whose body is on a platform above them.

called tipis. The Sioux were also skilled warriors for whom warfare was a way of life.

For the Sioux, warfare was the way a man gained status within his tribe. In a battle, each warrior fought on his own to try to achieve as many coups as possible. These were honors for bravery that were won by touching enemy warriors in battle. The greatest honor in battle was to kill an enemy in hand-to-hand combat.

" **Is it wrong for me to love my own? Is it wicked for me because my skin is red? Because I am Sioux? Because I was born where my father lived?** "

Sitting Bull

> ❝ We must act with earnestness against the Sioux even to their extermination, men, women, and children. ❞

General William T. Sherman, US Army, 1866

Settlers Push West

The Sioux had been fighting neighboring peoples on the Plains for nearly 200 years. After the end of the Civil War (1861–1865), however, they found themselves facing a new enemy. Growing numbers of white Americans were heading west in order to find land to farm or raise livestock. These settlers moved through the heart of Sioux territory as they made their way west toward Oregon or California. They expected the government in Washington, D.C., to protect them from the Sioux.

FORT: The US Army built forts on Sioux land, but most of the time relations were peaceful.

CONFLICT: Increasing settlement of the west brought whites into conflict with Native Americans.

Opposing Forces Gather

As westward expansion increased, the Sioux found themselves increasingly caught up in skirmishes with new settlers. Clashes between the two sides grew more violent. The government sent the US Army to protect the settlers. Among the soldiers who arrived was a veteran cavalry officer from the Civil War named George Armstrong Custer. Custer had become a hero in the Union for his aggressive tactics during the war. Meanwhile, Sitting Bull and other Sioux leaders became more determined to keep the settlers out of their territory. If necessary, they were prepared to fight the regular troops of the US Army to protect their ancestral lands.

SITTING BULL

Sitting Bull was a Lakota who became leader of all the Sioux. His reputation was based on his skill as a warrior and his wisdom as a holy man.

WARRIOR: Sitting Bull was a great warrior who led Sioux resistance to white settlement.

Sitting Bull was born near Grand River in South Dakota around 1831. He belonged to the Hunkpapa band of the Lakota, and his father and two of his uncles were tribal chiefs. His parents named him Jumping Badger.

Young Warrior

At the age of 10, Jumping Badger killed his first buffalo. At the age of 14, he earned his first coup. During a raid to steal horses, he touched a Crow warrior with a coup stick. This was a sign of great bravery. The boy's father was so proud that he renamed his son after himself, "Buffalo Bull Sits Down," shortened to Sitting Bull. Sitting Bull soon became a leader in Lakota fights with other native peoples. When the US Army attacked the Lakota in 1863, Sitting Bull fought back.

CAMP: This drawing shows Sitting Bull (right) and scenes of life on the Plains of Dakota.

A Spiritual Man

Sitting Bull was also a medicine man, who used magic to heal sickness. Medicine men could put themselves into trances in which they saw visions that were thought to be messages from the gods. The medicine men reported the messages to the rest of the band.

> " When I was a boy, the Sioux owned the world. The sun rose and set on their land; they sent ten thousand men to battle. Where are the warriors today? "

Sitting Bull

GENERAL CUSTER

» DASHING HERO

He was the most popular soldier in the United States, but after his death George Custer became a highly controversial figure.

HERO: Custer was known to be proud of his looks and confident about his own skills as a soldier.

Custer was born in New Rumley, Ohio, in December 1839. He went to the US Military Academy at West Point, but graduated at the bottom of his class. He collected so many demerits that his record is still one of the worst in the academy's history.

The Boy General

After leaving West Point, Custer joined the US Army. The Civil War was just beginning, and Custer had the chance to make his reputation. He served as a cavalry officer, and was involved in the first major battle of the war, the Battle of First Bull Run in July 1861. He even captured the first Confederate battle flag during the Battle of Gettysburg in 1863.

Custer was so successful that he was promoted temporarily to the rank of brigadier general in charge of volunteers at the age of just 23.

HUNTING: Custer (standing, center) loved hunting. Here he poses with guests on a hunting trip.

Custer also became popular with the general public for his good looks and battle heroics. He became known by his nickname of the "boy general." Custer's commander in the Civil War was Lieutenant General Philip Sheridan. He was a great admirer of the young officer.

After the war, Custer found it hard to achieve a similar level of success. He asked to fight for Mexico against an occupying army from France, but his superiors refused. The US Army's fight against Native Americans over land gave him a new focus. In 1866, Custer was appointed lieutenant colonel of the new 7th Cavalry Regiment.

> " I would be willing, yes glad, to see a battle every day during my life. "
>
> **George A. Custer**

WARRIOR STORY

» SIOUX LEADERS STAND AGAINST THE US ARMY

Despite Sitting Bull's leadership of the Sioux, he was just one of a generation of warriors who were determined to protect Sioux lands from settlers.

One of the first warriors to attack the US Army was a Lakota named Red Cloud (1822–1909), who had previously fought against the Pawnee and Crow. In what the US Army called Red Cloud's War, troops fought a series of clashes against an alliance of bands of Northern Cheyenne, Lakota, and Arapaho from 1866 to 1868.

One of the Lakota who took part in the Fetterman Massacre was Crazy Horse (c. 1842–1877). A great warrior, Crazy Horse played a key

RED CLOUD: Red Cloud gave his name to the conflicts known as Red Cloud's War.

WARRIOR: Gall, together with Crazy Horse, led the Sioux warriors at the Little Bighorn.

role in many battles between the Sioux and the US Army. Like Sitting Bull, Crazy Horse was determined to preserve the freedom of the Sioux against intervention by the US government.

Feared Warrior

The warrior Gall (c. 1840–1894) was another Hunkpapa Lakota. Sitting Bull and Gall fought together against the US Army. Gall later surrendered. He and his band moved to the Great Sioux Reservation.

> " I salute the light within your eyes where the whole Universe dwells. For when you are at that center within you and I am at that place within me, we shall be one. "

Crazy Horse speaks to
Sitting Bull, 1877

CUSTER'S BAND

Custer had many supporters among the military, particularly after his heroics during the Civil War. His most loyal supporter was his wife.

Among Custer's admirers was Major General Philip Sheridan, who later became general-in-chief of the US Army. In 1868, Sheridan recalled Custer to the army after he had been suspended for a year for being absent from duty. In 1876, shortly before the Battle of the Little Bighorn, President Ulysses S. Grant ordered Custer's arrest for leaving Washington, D.C., without permission. Grant was angry with Custer, who had accused Grant's brother and the Secretary of War of corruption for selling goods at army posts at high prices. Sheridan and General Alfred Terry persuaded Grant to reinstate Custer.

Indian Campaigns

Custer's fellow officers thought he was vain and unreliable. However, he did have some good friends in the 7th Cavalry Regiment.

GENERAL: Philip Sheridan first commanded Custer in the Civil War.

FAMILY: This photograph shows George Custer (left) with his wife Libbie and his younger brother, Tom.

They included Captain George W. Yates, who had served with Custer in the Civil War. Yates commanded E and F companies. Another friend who fought at Little Bighorn was Custer's brother-in-law James Calhoun, whom Custer had helped to gain promotion.

> **"A true cavalryman feels that a life in the saddle on the free open plain is his legitimate existence.**

Libbie Custer

Custer's younger brothers, Thomas and Boston, also served in the 7th Cavalry and later died at the Battle of the Little Bighorn. Custer's biggest supporter was his wife, Elizabeth Clift Bacon "Libbie" Custer.

LINES ARE DRAWN

The events that led to the Battle of the Little Bighorn began to unfold shortly after the end of the Civil War in 1865.

TRUCE: Custer, in his trademark tan buckskin jacket, negotiates a truce with native warriors.

After the war ended, a new wave of white Americans set out to settle in the West. Their growing numbers threatened the survival of many Native American peoples. Sitting Bull was determined to preserve his people's way of life, and his outspoken criticism of the settlers marked him as an important leader of the Lakota. In 1865 he led an attack on a new US fort, Fort Rice in North Dakota. His bravery in clashes with US troops and his authority as a spiritual guide for his people led him to be made chief of the Lakota around 1868. The following year, he was made the supreme chief of the Sioux people, which made him a target for the US government.

CHARGE: Men of Custer's 7th Cavalry training to use their swords.

Custer in the Cavalry

In December 1866, George Custer moved to Fort Riley, Kansas, to take command of the 7th Cavalry Regiment, which had been set up to protect settlers. On November 27, 1868, Custer led an attack on a Cheyenne camp on the Washita River, in what is now Oklahoma. More than 100 Cheyenne men, women, and children died. Custer was criticized for abandoning a small group of troopers on the battlefield. They were among the 21 soldiers who died.

> " Squaws and children . . . had been slain in the excitement and confusion of the first charge. "
>
> Custer, Report on the Battle of Washita, December 22, 1868

DIVISIVE TREATIES

The US government tried to force the Sioux to give up their land in two treaties signed at Fort Laramie in what is now Wyoming.

In 1851 the US government had signed the first Treaty of Fort Laramie with tribes living on the Plains, including the Sioux and others. The treaty defined the territory of each tribe. In exchange for an annual payment of $50,000, each tribe had agreed to allow settlers to pass across its land. The 1851 treaty soon became unworkable as thousands of white settlers moved to the Plains.

In 1868, the government agreed to a second Treaty of Fort Laramie with the Sioux. This time it was designed to bring peace between the

REPRESENTATIVES: Members of the Sioux gather at Fort Laramie in 1868.

HILLS: The Great Sioux Reservation included the Black Hills of Dakota.

settlers and the Sioux. The treaty tried to force the Sioux to settle permanently on a reservation in what is now South Dakota. The Sioux would still be able to roam to hunt buffalo across the Plains, however. This second Fort Laramie agreement had far-reaching consequences. Sitting Bull and other Sioux leaders rejected its terms. They urged the Sioux not to move to the reservation.

> " The government of the United States desires peace, and its honor is hereby pledged to keep it. The Indians desire peace, and they now pledge their honor to maintain it. "

Transcript of Treaty of Laramie, 1868

HONSINGER BLUFF

On August 4, 1873, Custer's 7th Cavalry clashed with Sitting Bull for the first time, with grave consequences for Custer's future.

The clash, known as the Battle of Honsinger Bluff, took place on the Yellowstone River in eastern Montana. Custer and the 7th Cavalry were in the area to protect surveyors from the Northern Pacific Railway from possible Native American attack. The company was planning the third transcontinental railroad in the United States. The line was planned to pass through Sioux territory.

First Clash

With little sign of any Sioux, Custer left the surveyors to take his men hunting. On August 4, Custer and a small party of soldiers were attacked by a group of Sioux warriors led by Crazy Horse and Sitting Bull. The young Sioux had not planned the attack well. Custer and his men were able to fight off the warriors. Just one warrior and one soldier were killed in the fight.

SCOUTS: Custer (seated) with his scouts on the 1873 Yellowstone Expedition.

SIOUX: Custer's Sioux scout, Bloody Knife, was bullied as a child. He deserted his tribe to serve the US Army.

Increasing Significance

The clash at Honsinger Bluff was not seen as being particularly important at the time. It took on greater significance three years later, after the battle at Little Bighorn. Some historians believe that this first encounter led Custer to underestimate the fighting skill of Sitting Bull, Crazy Horse, and their warriors. The brief fight confirmed Custer's belief that the Sioux were more likely to flee from trouble rather than fight. This would prove a fatal mistake.

> " The abundant preparation which the Yellowstone Expedition made for the reception of the Indians has been fully justified. "

Evansville Daily Journal, Indiana, August 26, 1873

THE BLACK HILLS

In the summer of 1874, the US Army sent 1,000 men under Custer's command to explore the Black Hills in Sioux territory.

EXPEDITION: Custer's expedition arrived in the Black Hills with about 1,000 men and 110 wagons.

The official purpose of Custer's expedition was to find a suitable location for a new US military post in Sioux territory. However, its real purpose was to investigate rumors that the Black Hills held rich deposits of gold. Custer reported in the *New York Times* that there was indeed gold in the hills, although he exaggerated the amount.

Miners Arrive

Custer did not mention that the land belonged to the Sioux. Indeed, the Black Hills were sacred to the Sioux. They believed the hills, which they called Paha Sapa, were the site of the tribe's creation.

SETTLEMENT: Log cabins built by miners crowd Deadwood Gulch in the Black Hills.

Lured by the promise of gold, prospectors flocked to the Black Hills. By the fall of 1875, there were 15,000 miners in the region. The US government tried to buy the Black Hills from the Sioux for $6 million. Sitting Bull refused, but the government did nothing to stop miners from flooding into Sioux territory. It became clear that Sitting Bull's resistance was potentially a major obstacle to the interests of the US government in the West. Other native peoples who had not yet ceded their territory to the United States were also seen as trouble.

> **We have discovered a rich and beautiful land.**

Custer writes to his wife Libbie, July 18, 1874

RESERVATION ORDER

To solve the problem of removing the Sioux from the lands they legally owned, the Office of Indian Affairs came up with a solution.

HUNT: The buffalo hunt from October until April took the Sioux right across the Plains.

The Office of Indian Affairs wanted to stop the Sioux from roaming freely on the Plains. On December 6, 1875, it ordered all Sioux to return to the Great Sioux Reservation in South Dakota by January 31, 1876. If the Sioux failed to comply, they would be treated as being "hostile." That would mean they were enemies of the United States.

An Impossible Order

Many Sioux were hunting buffalo far from the reservation. It was almost impossible for them to reach the reservation in time for the deadline. Many others simply did not want to go to the reservation.

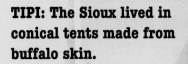

TIPI: The Sioux lived in conical tents made from buffalo skin.

These nomadic Sioux were in the middle of their hunting season, so they had enough buffalo supplies for the winter. The Great Sioux Reservation itself, meanwhile, was suffering from a shortage of food. Famine drove many Sioux from the reservation to wander the Plains.

When the January 31 deadline came, it was clear that the Sioux had not obeyed the government's order. General Philip H. Sheridan ordered Generals Alfred H. Terry and George R. Crook to begin a campaign against the "hostiles." They were to force the Sioux and their allies, the Northern Cheyenne, to move back to the reservation.

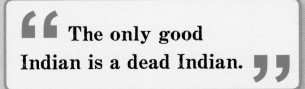

" The only good Indian is a dead Indian. "

General Philip H. Sheridan

SITTING BULL'S VISION

When the Sioux did not return to their reservation by the end of January 1876, the US government declared war on them.

On February 8, 1876, General Philip Sheridan sent a telegraph message to Generals George R. Crook and Alfred H. Terry. He ordered them to attack the Sioux and their allies. Crook launched the first attack at the Battle of Powder River. On March 17, 1876, he ordered Colonel Joseph J. Reynolds to attack a Cheyenne village on Powder River in what is now Montana. The cavalry attack was poorly planned. Different army companies became separated or lost. Nevertheless, over the course of about five hours the soldiers were able to destroy much of the Cheyenne village and the possessions of the villagers.

The biggest effect of this first battle was to turn the opinion of Sitting Bull and the other native leaders against the United States and government attempts to seize Sioux territory.

REYNOLDS: Joseph J. Reynolds led the attack on the Powder River.

DANCE: The Sioux believed the Sun Dance allowed them to communicate with the "Great Spirit."

The Sun Dance

Early in June 1876, a large group of Sioux and Northern Cheyenne gathered on Rosebud Creek in Montana Territory for the annual Sun Dance. The dance was the most important of all the Sioux spiritual ceremonies. People fasted, danced, and prayed to the "Great Spirit," Wakan Tanka. Sitting Bull cut pieces of flesh from his arms as a form of sacrifice. He then fell into a trance. When he awoke he said he had experienced a vision in which he saw many US soldiers falling from the sky like grasshoppers. The Sioux took this to be a prophecy of a victory over the "Long Knives," the name they used to describe the US cavalry.

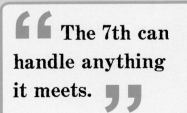

" The 7th can handle anything it meets. "

George Custer

TOWARD BATTLE

Sitting Bull's vision of the defeat of the US soldiers during the Sun Dance drew other allies to join the Sioux.

After the Sun Dance, the Sioux moved south. More Sioux, Northern Cheyenne, and Arapaho joined the new camp because of Sitting Bull's prophecy. Meanwhile, the US Army was ready to start rounding up the Sioux. In June 1876, armies led by General Alfred Terry and Colonel John Gibbon met at the Yellowstone River to launch a two-pronged advance on the Sioux camp. Gibbon's men were ordered to march up the Little Bighorn River, while Custer's orders were to march around the Wolf Mountains.

OFFICERS: Officers of the 7th Cavalry prepare a meal in their tent while on campaign.

ROSEBUD: Crazy Horse's warriors attack US soldiers on Rosebud Creek.

Battle of the Rosebud

On June 17, 1876. Crazy Horse led around 1,000 Cheyenne and Lakota warriors in an attack on General Crook's column of soldiers at a bend in Rosebud Creek. The two sides fought for around six hours. The native warriors attacked the US Army positions again and again.

Eventually, it was Crazy Horse who gave up the fight and withdrew. Crook claimed a victory, but he was highly alarmed by the aggression and determination of the enemy. He withdrew his men from the area. This would have important consequences for the Battle of the Little Bighorn.

> **These dead soldiers are the gifts of Wakan Tanka. Kill them, but do not take their guns or horses.**

Sitting Bull talking about his vision

AT LITTLE BIGHORN

Custer's orders to march around the Wolf Mountains were clear, but he ignored them. This decision left him separated from the other US forces.

Instead of marching his men around the Wolf Mountains, Custer instead led them straight through the hilly region. The men covered 76 miles (122 km) in three days, and were exhausted. They reached the Sioux camp on the Little Bighorn River before the other prong of the advance, but Custer planned to attack anyway. He divided his 600 men into three units. He commanded one, another was under the command of Major Marcus Reno, and Captain Frederick Benteen commanded the third. Custer's unit numbered around 268 men.

CAMP: The Little Bighorn River was a traditional site for Native American encampments.

WARRIORS: This painting by a native artist shows Sioux warriors at Little Bighorn.

Custer Makes His Attack

Custer's native scouts warned him that the Sioux encampment was much larger than they had believed, but Custer ignored them. He ordered Reno to attack the camp from the south while Benteen went scouting. Custer took his men to mount a surprise attack on the camp from the north. Reno's men launched an attack but were fought off and fled to a nearby forest.

> **" Any of you men who wish to live, make your escape! Follow me! "**
>
> **Major Marcus Reno, Battle of the Little Bighorn**

Sitting Bull had intended to make peace with the soldiers, but changed his mind after his favorite horse was shot. Spotting Custer's men to the north, the Sioux warriors set out to face them.

THE LAST STAND

When the Sioux spotted Custer's unit on open ground overlooking the Little Bighorn River, they saw an opportunity for victory.

CUT OFF: Sioux warriors surrounded Custer and his men, making escape impossible.

Custer also hoped to win a victory, even after Reno's men were driven from the battle. He remembered the Battle of Washita in 1873, when Crazy Horse and Sitting Bull had fled from his small force of soldiers. He expected the Sioux to flee again. Instead, up to 7,000 warriors led by Crazy Horse advanced, forcing Custer to retreat to the top of a hill. Sioux warriors crawled through the long grass, surprising the soldiers. (The Sioux called the fight the Battle of the Greasy Grass.) The soldiers dismounted to fight.

HERO: Custer fights bravely on in this romanticized illustration of the Last Stand.

Death of a Hero

By the time Custer reached what became known as Last Stand Hill, fewer than 100 US soldiers survived. They fought on but were hugely outnumbered. Sioux witnesses later reported that every one of Custer's men was dead within an hour. The Sioux then regrouped to attack the soldiers on lower ground led by Reno and Benteen, but those soldiers fought them off for the rest of the day and most of the next. The Sioux withdrew when General Alfred Terry eventually arrived with US reinforcements.

> " Soldiers were piled up one on top of another, dead, and here and there an Indian among the soldiers. "

Runs the Enemy, warrior of the Two Kettle tribe, Battle of Little Bighorn

THE OLD CHIEF

The victory at the Little Bighorn marked the peak of Sitting Bull's power and the high point of the Sioux's battle against the United States.

Custer's defeat made the US government even more determined to defeat the Sioux. The government stepped up its efforts to drive the Sioux from their sacred lands by ordering the slaughter of all buffalo. Sitting Bull and his followers retreated to Canada in the spring of 1877. He stayed there for four years, but a lack of buffalo made the Sioux lifestyle difficult. In 1881, he returned and surrendered to the United States. He moved to the Standing Rock Reservation in North Dakota in 1883.

SHOWMAN: Sitting Bull poses with Buffalo Bill Cody during his time with the Wild West Show in 1885.

Wild West Show

In 1885, Sitting Bull joined the successful Wild West Show of Buffalo Bill Cody. Sitting Bull and his warriors rode around the arena and were a popular attraction.

DEATH: This Sioux drawing shows Sitting Bull (center, in white) being shot by a policeman.

He earned $50 a week and could charge as much as $2 for his autograph. However, after four months, Sitting Bull returned to the reservation. There, he had a vision that his own people would kill him. In 1890 a movement called the Ghost Dance spread through native peoples on the Plains. It promised the defeat of the whites. The government was worried Sitting Bull would encourage such beliefs to spread. It sent Lakota police to arrest him. On December 15, 1890, Sitting Bull was killed in a gunfight.

> " I, Takanka Iyotanka, I wish it to be remembered that I was the last man of my tribe to surrender my rifle. "

Sitting Bull on his return to the United States from Canada, 1881

A FALLEN HERO

Despite his defeat, the Battle of the Little Bighorn was General Custer's finest hour. Americans were shocked to hear of his death.

General Terry and his men arrived two days after the battle had ended. Terry buried Custer alongside Custer's brother, Tom, who had also died in the battle. News of Custer's death caused great shock. Reports and paintings of the "Last Stand" became popular, and Custer was seen as a national hero and a martyr.

REBURIAL: A year after his death, Custer was reburied with military honors at West Point.

A man too big for legend—
A motion picture
too big
for any screen
except
CINERAMA

CINERAMA
presents
ROBERT SHAW
as
CUSTER
OF THE
WEST

MOVIE: Custer has been portrayed many times in movies. This poster is from a Hollywood film made in 1967.

Making of a Myth

Custer's wife, Libbie, helped to keep the story of her husband's heroism alive by writing a series of books. Two of the few people to criticize Custer's tactics were President Ulysses S. Grant and Custer's commanding officer, General Philip Sheridan. It was not until a century later that the truth about his disastrous tactics became widely known.

> " Hurrah boys, we've got them! We'll finish them up and then go home to our station. "

Custer supposedly said these words shortly before he was killed.

AFTERMATH

The Sioux victory at the Battle of the Little Bighorn marked a turning point in Native American attempts to protect their territory.

The deaths of Custer and his men only increased the view among most Americans that Native Americans were "savages." The US government stepped up its efforts to seize Native American territory.

End of Sioux Resistance

One native response was the Ghost Dance. The movement began in 1890 when a Northern Paiute seer named Wovoka had a vision that ritual dances would bring unity and victory to the Plains peoples. Brigadier General Nelson A. Miles was worried that the movement would encourage Sitting Bull to lead another uprising. He ordered

CAMP: This was the Sioux camp shortly before the massacre at Wounded Knee.

40

GRAVE: Dead Sioux are buried after being killed by US cavalry at Wounded Knee.

Sitting Bull's arrest at the Standing Rock reservation, which led to Sitting Bull's death during a gunfight with police. A chief named Big Foot took his place as leader of the Sioux.

On December 29, 1890, the 7th Cavalry had Big Foot's band of warriors surrounded near Wounded Knee creek in South Dakota. As the cavalry tried to disarm the outnumbered Sioux, a shot was fired. The cavalry began firing wildly, killing more than 200 men, women, and children. After the massacre, the Sioux would never again be a military threat to the United States.

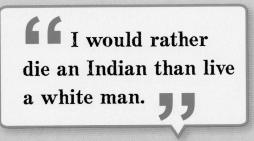

" I would rather die an Indian than live a white man. "

Sitting Bull

JUDGMENT

SITTING BULL Vs. GEORGE ARMSTRONG CUSTER

Sitting Bull is no longer seen as having been an enemy of the United States. Many Americans now regret the treatment of the Sioux in the 19th century.

* Sitting Bull wanted to maintain the Sioux's traditional life hunting buffalo, but by the 19th century this was impossible.

* Sitting Bull was prepared to meet violence with violence after his favorite horse was shot.

* Sitting Bull and his warriors knew their way of life was under threat at Little Bighorn, which is why they fought so hard.

* Sitting Bull and Custer clashed directly on just two occasions: at the Battle of Washita and the Battle of the Little Bighorn.

Since his death at Little Bighorn, General Custer's reputation has descended from being that of a hero to being that of a reckless leader who led his men to their deaths.

* During the Civil War, Custer's exploits made him a national hero.

* After the Civil War, Custer was eager to become the nation's leading Indian hunter.

* After the Battle of Washita, Custer assumed Sioux warriors would flee and scatter during battle.

* Custer's reputation as a hero was helped by the books written about him by his widow, Libbie.

TIMELINE

Although Sitting Bull and George A. Custer only clashed twice on the battlefield, they were rivals for over a decade as they embodied the struggle between the Plains Indians and the US government.

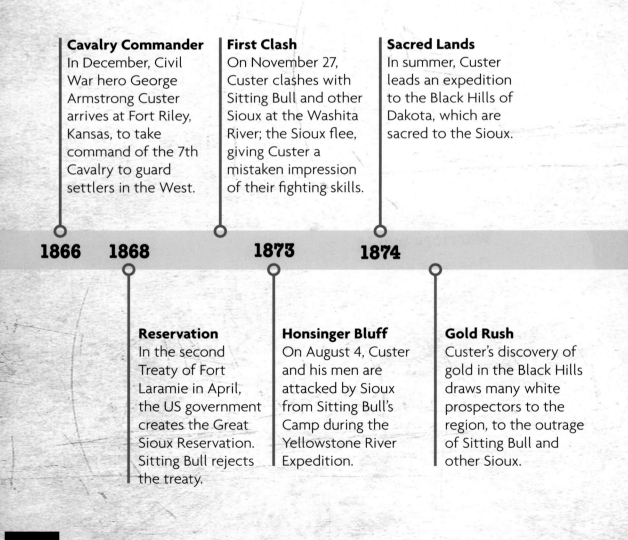

Cavalry Commander
In December, Civil War hero George Armstrong Custer arrives at Fort Riley, Kansas, to take command of the 7th Cavalry to guard settlers in the West.

First Clash
On November 27, Custer clashes with Sitting Bull and other Sioux at the Washita River; the Sioux flee, giving Custer a mistaken impression of their fighting skills.

Sacred Lands
In summer, Custer leads an expedition to the Black Hills of Dakota, which are sacred to the Sioux.

1866   1868   1873   1874

Reservation
In the second Treaty of Fort Laramie in April, the US government creates the Great Sioux Reservation. Sitting Bull rejects the treaty.

Honsinger Bluff
On August 4, Custer and his men are attacked by Sioux from Sitting Bull's Camp during the Yellowstone River Expedition.

Gold Rush
Custer's discovery of gold in the Black Hills draws many white prospectors to the region, to the outrage of Sitting Bull and other Sioux.

SITTING BULL Vs. GEORGE ARMSTRONG CUSTER

Reservation Order
In November, the US government orders all Sioux not living on the Great Sioux Reservation to move there by January 31, 1876; many Sioux ignore the order.

Powder River
On March 17, US forces attack and destroy a Cheyenne encampment on the Powder River in Montana, starting the Great Sioux War.

US Withdrawal
Sioux resistance in the Battle of the Rosebud on June 17 is so fierce that General George Crook withdraws his men, weakening US forces in the area.

1875 1876

Hostile Status
When the January 31 deadline passes, Sioux living outside the Great Sioux Reservation are classified as "hostiles."

Powerful Vision
At the annual Sun Dance in June, Sitting Bull has a vision that he interprets as promising Sioux victory over the US soldiers. Other Native Americans join his band.

Last Stand
Custer and his whole command die after a poorly planned attack on a large Sioux encampment on the Little Bighorn River in what is now Montana.

GLOSSARY

allies Different people, groups, or nations who agree to work together to achieve a shared goal.

cavalry Soldiers who fight on horseback.

ceded Describes something that has been given up.

Confederate Related to the Confederate States of America, formed by the Southern states during the Civil War.

coups Among Plains peoples, honors gained for feats of bravery that involve touching an enemy warrior in battle without being harmed.

demerits Marks awarded against someone for faults or failures.

famine A period of extreme shortage of food.

Great Spirit For the Sioux, the Great Spirit was the most important deity.

hostilities Acts of warfare.

massacre The killing of many people, who are usually unarmed or poorly armed.

medicine man A person believed to have magical powers of healing.

morale The confidence and positive feelings of a person or group.

nomadic Wandering around rather than living in a single place.

prophecy A prediction of something that will happen in the future.

prospectors People who are looking for deposits of minerals, such as gold.

reservation An area set aside for the use of a particular Native American people.

sacrifice To give up something as an offering, particularly to a god.

scouting Gathering information about an area or about movements of an enemy.

seer A person said to have a supernatural ability to see the future.

skirmish A small-scale clash between armed forces.

surveyors People who examine the land, usually to establish ownership or in preparation for construction work.

tactics The organization of forces on the battlefield in order to achieve victory.

tipis Conical tents made by stretching animal hide over a wooden framework.

trance A state in which someone is only half conscious.

truce A temporary halt to fighting arranged during a war.

Union The Northern states during the Civil War.

visions Dreamlike experiences that take place during a trance.

Westward expansion The spread of US government and settlement west of the Mississippi River in the 19th century.

FOR FURTHER INFORMATION

Books

Dunn, Joeming W., and Ben Dunn. *Custer's Last Stand* (Graphic History). Magic Wagon, 2008.

Fradin, Dennis Brindell. *Custer's Last Stand* (Turning Points in US History). Cavendish Square Publishing, 2006.

Hamilton, John. *Battle of Little Bighorn* (Great Battles). ABDO and Daughters, 2014.

Reis, Ronald A. *Sitting Bull* (Legends of the Wild West). Chelsea House Publishing, 2010.

Sanford, William R. *Hunkpapa Lakota Chief Sitting Bull* (Native American Chiefs and Warriors). Enslow Publishing, 2013.

Spinner, Stephanie. *Who Was Sitting Bull?* Turtleback Books, 2014.

Websites

www.californiaindianeducation.org/famous_indian_chiefs/sitting_bull/
A page about Sitting Bull from the California Indian Education.

www.eyewitnesstohistory.com/custer.htm
An eyewitness account of the Battle of the Little Bighorn by George Herendon, a scout serving with Major Reno.

www.pbs.org/weta/thewest/people/s_z/sittingbull.htm
PBS biography of Sitting Bull, with links to many other articles.

www.historynet.com/sitting-bull
History Net's biography of Sitting Bull.

http://www.americaslibrary.gov/jb/recon/jb_recon_custer_1.html
America's Story describes the lead-up to the Battle of the Little Bighorn.

http://www.slideshare.net/HenrikJensen4/sitting-bull-vs-general-custer
A page of collected quotes from Sitting Bull and General Custer.

Publisher's note to educators and parents: Our editors have carefully reviewed these websites to ensure that they are suitable for students. Many websites change frequently, however, and we cannot guarantee that a site's future contents will continue to meet our high standards of quality and educational value. Be advised that students should be closely supervised whenever they access the Internet.

INDEX